greenspace

a collection of poems

Christina Lee

Copyright © 2021 by Christina H. Lee

All rights reserved. No part of this book may be reproduced or used in any manner without written permission of the copyright owner except for the use of quotations in a book review.

First Edition February 2021

Book cover by Rozlyn Dubz

ISBN: 978-1-09836-637-7

*for all the diamonds
lost at the bottom of the ocean*

*i hope these words find you
and lift you up
and out
and over*

Content Warning:
Depression
Anxiety
Substance abuse

TABLE OF CONTENTS

volume i: panacea

inner child | **1**
dear abby | **9**
dear rebecca | **13**
reveal, part i | **17**
reveal, part ii | **19**
reveal, part iii | **20**
reveal, part iv | **21**
reveal, part v | **23**
frostbite | **25**
mufasa | **29**
asking for a friend | **33**
to whom it may concern | **37**
gasoline | **41**
cloth mother | **47**
fill in the | **51**
quiver | **55**
war | **59**
beansprout | **61**

volume ii: metamorphosis

tread softly | **67**
you're a wizard, harry | **69**
the sky | **71**
cannabis | **73**
galaxy, part i | **81**
galaxy, part ii | **83**
maybe a forest is a better metaphor | **85**
a fantasy | **87**
breadcrumbs | **89**
is this poem about drugs or him | **93**
imprisoned | **95**
dark chocolate | **96**
volcano | **97**
snake | **103**
canyon | **105**
dear me, part i | **107**
dear me, part ii | **109**
carbon | **111**
myself | **115**
greenspace | **117**
transformation | **121**

acknowledgements | **125**
about the author | **127**

VOLUME I:

PANACEA

INNER CHILD

hello, little me
at this point in your life
things may seem
a little bleak
there is a persistent
buzz of worry
dense static
inside and around you
and most of the time
you don't even know why
let me tell you
it's all in your head
don't get me wrong—
that doesn't mean it's not real
but you control it
not the other way around
so embrace the chaos
because one day
that endless noise will
be quiet
and the traces of those dark thoughts
like primitive charcoal smudges
will form a beautiful mural
of all the battles you fought
and won

hello, little one
right now it feels like
no one understands you
like you are a diamond
lost at the bottom of the sea
shining your light into
endless darkness
but don't worry because
i know where to find you
i see you
i see you
the only reason you're down there
is because you need to
get used to
your own light first
before you can be a light unto others
so there's nothing to worry about
because i will pull ourselves up
from the depths
once you're ready
to shine

hello, little you
sometimes it feels like a storm
inside your little heart
that organ in your chest feels
too much

"too sensitive"
"too touchy"
"too dramatic"
"too hurt"
it's okay
just feel
let the storm rage
because after the rain
the lightning will clarify
a scar on your forehead, which means
you're special
you're a wizard
of emotion
thunder, it breaks
    it re-creates
molecules into atoms
your thunder creates depths
that others will never travel
how do you think
you got all the way down there
at the bottom of the ocean?
you have enough breadth to endure
lightning strikes
so feel it all, little one
and one day, your little heart
will grow big enough
to hold all the love
you could ever imagine

hello, littlest
take a small step forward
i promise it will be okay
i'm already ahead of you
guiding the way
so take a step
and then another
stray from the path
if you are feeling brave
you'll find another one
just as long as you keep
stepping forward

guess what, little child
you can do what you want
dye your hair if you want to
chop it off if it feels right
(it does)
rebel from your parents' expectations
because eventually, they will understand
     and eventually, you will understand them, too
don't let anyone else tell you
how to live your life
yes, take heed of your elders
but remember
the only wisdom you will acquire
is the kind you plant and sow
all on your own

my dear, sweet child
while you're still there
at the bottom of the ocean
there is a secret you keep
      a pain
      a shame so dark
you are afraid to bring it out
      into the light
you are afraid that if you do
the storm that comes after
will break everything
you've ever loved
you think it's easier
to bear this pain alone
that no good will come from
exposing the weakest parts of you
and maybe you're right
      maybe for now, it's okay
      to hide that pain away
i understand
and it is with compassion that i say
you are wrong
this kind of pain only grows stronger
in the dark
the only way to heal this
is to shine a spotlight
directly on the part that hurts

let me warn you
at first, it may feel like
the storm
is more than you can handle
but one day, when you are almost ready
to step into—
and out of—
the darkness
you will go to california
to see the redwoods
those ancient trees you've always wanted
to crane your neck to see
you will stand amongst living giants
their roots bursting up from
the bottom of the ocean
and you will finally breathe
those mighty trees are strong
    not because they're tall
    not because they stand alone
but because their roots are connected down below
    and if you want to take one down
    you gotta take the whole damn forest
i know you're afraid
i know you're hurting
but one day, we will be strong enough to say:
    enough is enough
    i will not bear this pain alone.

goodbye, little one
one more thing before i go
the secret to life is that
happiness isn't a place
there is no door
        no secret platform in between
telling you, surprise!
you've arrived!
the surprise is
you're already here
there
everywhere
anywhere
you must look inside
surprise!
did it sneak up on you?
don't let it sneak away
happiness is a choice
a yes or a no
just like pain
you've got to let the happiness out
but unlike pain
happiness only thrives
if you bring it out
into the light

so let it shine, little one
be the diamond in the dark

because one day
we will be strong enough
to pull ourselves out
into the light

DEAR ABBY,

i know you're younger
but in age only
i've always looked up to you
and all the things you do
do you know how many new things
you've taught me?

don't ever sell yourself short
because you are your own biggest critic
everyone else thinks

you're a wonder

but anyway, who cares what
everyone else thinks
the only person you should impress
is yourself

open your eyes
and see yourself clearly
you're one bad ass woman
best older sister
my surrogate mother
future surgeon and

you know you're my hero, right?

christina lee

i respect you the most in my life
so get on my level
and respect yourself the most

you are deserving
of every little thing
you've ever wanted
someone to nurture you
as you nurture others
a big house on a farm
away from the people who
annoy the shit out of you
having someone else cook for once
and not having to pretend that it tastes good
you deserve rest
whenever you want it
though i know
you will only take what you need
too many new projects
    pouches to sew
    breads to bake
    jams to prepare
    mouths to feed
    people to save

you know you're my hero, right?

never worry about being
"too sharp"
because a dulled blade
is no use to anyone
unsheathe that sword
strike with precision
skim the fat
skin the beast
excise the heart of the matter
be the sharp blade that you are
because exquisite craftsmanship
should never be hidden away
inside a sheath made to protect those
who don't have the expertise to handle
such a weapon

i don't say it enough but
i love you.
i appreciate you.
thank you.
be kind to yourself.
be understanding.
and take the time to do things that you love
because nothing is more wonderful
than watching you do
something you enjoy

i'm blessed to call you my sister
i'm blessed to have felt the sting of your blade
because i know you will also
go to war for me if i asked
keep being you
forget what anyone else thinks
because you are the only person
who needs to like you

and now we've come to
a fork in the road
where i will have to be strong enough
to let you go
you will always be
the voice of reason in my head
the backup when i'm scared
the friend when i had none
the support to hold me up when
i couldn't do it alone
and i'm so grateful to have a sister who
loves as fiercely as you do

you know you're my hero, right?

DEAR REBECCA,

remember when
you used to cling to my leg
and beg me to
take you on all my adventures?

well, it seems
the tables have turned
and here i am
waving as you leave

the world is at your feet
but there's a bit of a jump
i don't know how far down
are you brave enough?
silly question—of course you are!

because you're a lion
a huntress who always gets her prey
because you're a tiger
graceful and terrifying
because you're a bear
protective of anyone lucky enough
to be called your cubs

you are fierce and soft
a cactus who thrives in the driest sands

but inside is all water
giving life to any who know
how to get past your bristles
you're a burnt marshmallow
gooey sweetness surrounded by
crusty burns
you've withstood the fire
you've transformed into something magical
savor the crunch, relish the smooth

and when things get hard
when you feel like crying because
you're carrying your worries on your shoulders
like Atlas at the end of the world
remember to take a minute
to appreciate where you are
how far you've come
and that you are

the bravest person i know

be a trailblazer
light the world on fire
if you must

live like the world is your hair
paint it bright and bold
in all your favorite colors

don't be afraid to
make mistakes
because if your hair falls out
you can always shave it off and start fresh

you really are
the bravest person i know

go where we've never gone before
lead the way
hold the torch
discover new places
but you can only do that if you
                                      jump—
remember i said you'd have to be brave?

trust that you will know
when you've found whatever your heart
was searching for
it's out there somewhere
but you may need to
color outside the lines
read between the lines
go beyond the confines
of your comfort zone

i admire you
because you are unafraid

to be who you are
to live as loud as you want
as bright as you choose
as ferociously as
the bravest tiger

i'd say i'm proud of you
but that wouldn't be fair
because i had nothing to do with
the woman you've become
you've long outgrown me
it's finally time
for you to let go of my leg
it's time for you
to find a new place to land

i love you
more than a mother loves her cubs

be proud
tilt your chin up to the sky
and remember to breathe

i'll be here
when you return from your adventures
tending the fire and keeping your spot warm

REVEAL, PART I

you reveal yourself
in the way you speak

you are what you say you are
and what you don't say

you expose yourself
in the twitch of the lip
a laugh that booms so deep
i could get lost
in those torturous caverns

your words, they are
to the point
and i kinda
like it
i like the pause before they come
like a cliché
calm before the

storm
you reveal yourself

in your slow approach
the way you skirt around
all the edges

i know what you crave
by the clear outlines where
words don't exist
saying exactly
what you don't say

you try to conceal
but you reveal yourself
instead

REVEAL, PART II

did you know
you make me smile?

unexpected
but i like it

REVEAL, PART III

please refrain
from whispering
in my ear
the echoes are
far too loud
in the hollows where

the slumbering beast
sleeps

i did not expect you
to be the one
to wake it up

REVEAL, PART IV

curious, how
you showed me something
about my soul
i didn't know existed
it only took one look from you
to open my eyes to
the parts of me
i didn't want to see

my soul, it has long felt
uncomfortable
inside this hollow chest
it only took one look from you
to see right through me

you showed me
that my soul doesn't like the cold
so it ran to the sun
    it found its place within my skin
so thin
exposed to the
elements
emotions
extremities of life

you showed me
that my soul is
    raw
    burnt
that there's a reason
everyone else's souls
live on the inside
but i have since learned
how to fill the spaces where
the sleeves were once too big
for my shoulders

you showed me
that i must keep searching
for those hollow spaces

REVEAL, PART V

don't ask me to undress
i'm already exposed
i reveal myself
in the way i speak
    the way i write
    the way i smile or don't
    the way i
        fall silent

i expose myself
in the way i can't look you in the eye
you will learn more about me
by reading the gaps in my soul
see how raw and blistered
how it burns and bristles
from the ultraviolet stares
of everyone who wants to see
underneath

so please
don't ask me to undress
before you can envision
what my soul would look like
complete, a masterpiece
    yes, i'm a masterpiece
but i'm not done yet

imagine me atop a pedestal
see the potential in me
see past the gaps and fill them
with your fantasies
so excuse me
if it takes a while
to reveal my work-in-progress
like i said before
it's more than just my heart on my sleeve
it's my soul on my skin
exposed
so please don't touch
until i trust you not to break
the pieces held together by glue

don't ask me to undress
until you've proven
that you're as incomplete as me

this is what it's like
inside my soul

FROSTBITE

i will not apologize
for who i am

i've got thick walls
made of ice
you're lucky you got past
so don't complain
if what you find inside
doesn't match
what you expected of me

there were warning signs
a pincer raised
a rattle shaken
so don't come crying
if you get stung
for overstepping

and please, don't come to me
for the antidote

i won't apologize
for the bite of my heart

but i will be fair
if you are

i will respect your boundaries
if you respect mine
don't push at the ice
because you'll only get frostbite
you already know
the best way in
is a small flame
held close
pressed up to the thinnest part of me

you've got to know
i bruise easy
the ice is not to keep you out
but to keep me from hurting myself
on other people's edges
i'm working on keeping the ice back
but all i've got is
a small flame
held close
pressed up to the thickest parts of me
i'm trying to melt it down

i'm not asking you to wait
but if you do
one day, these walls will fall
and there you'll be
holding a small flame

it will fit perfectly
in the hollows
of my frigid
thawing
heart

warm, at last

MUFASA

letting go
isn't as easy
as opening up your hand

let go, you whisper
but i'm certain that i've tried
would i be here now, white-knuckled
still hanging on
if i had succeeded in
letting go?

let go of certainty, you say
but it's not that simple
when certainty, with its iron-clad claws
is the only thing keeping me from
falling off this cliff

would i need your
unsolicited advice
if i hadn't already tried
unclenching my fist?

it doesn't work like that
but thank you
for prying your way
between my tired fingers

you, for whom i had already
loosened my grip

but i guess that wasn't enough

don't criticize
when you haven't felt
the sharp teeth gnawing
at the soft tissues in your head
don't speak
about my pain
as if it's something i can just
let go
as if i haven't already tried
on my own

if you want me to
let go
just to let you in
you better be sure
you are strong enough
to pull me up

but, don't worry
i don't need or want you to save me
i will pull myself up off this cliff
even if you are standing above me
telling me to—

let go

ASKING FOR A FRIEND

how do you fill
a black hole?

i'm asking for a friend
cause they once told me
that that's what it feels like
inside their heart
a black hole
a supermassive entity
consuming every happy thing
they've ever tried to love

did you know
an atom is mostly
empty space
a precarious dance
of electrons
orbiting a nucleus
atoms are mostly empty
and we are made of atoms
but somehow that makes us whole
solid
we are matter
we matter

but some days,
my friend feels like
an atom about to collapse
like they are full of
empty space

some days,
they would say,
i feel like i am more space
than matter

how do you satisfy
the insatiable pull of
a black hole?

i'm asking for a friend
you see, they told me
sometimes they will sit in the sun
and pray that somehow
this chill inside of them
will finally be warm
when will i be warm?
(said my friend, not me)
do you think the sun has enough heat
to fill this void inside of me?

so if you ever find out the answer
please let me know
so i can pass it on
to my friend

how do you fill
a black hole?

TO WHOM IT MAY CONCERN

you're going through something
some heartbreak
some unnamed distress

i remember what it's like
living under that dense fog
that invades your thoughts
and covers everything in
a scratchy woollen blanket
it makes your tongue
reek of decay
so food tastes like ash
and all the things you love
suddenly feel like
the most trivial things in the world

i remember what it's like
to be an atom
about to collapse

i remember what it's like
to stay in bed all day
to disappear into the valleys of your duvet
because nothing is hard
in a bed made of feathers

it's okay

i remember what it's like
take your time
heal your heart
clear your mind
of all those worries—
maybe they're real
but so are flecks of dust
floating in a ray of sun
they're real, but
insubstantial

i'm sorry for the pain you feel
i remember what it's like
for your heart to work so hard
to keep pumping iron
just to keep you from falling

i am sending you
all my love
so that you might
remember what it's like
to feel joy explode from your lungs
in a burst of laughter

i am sending you
all my love

so you'll know
there's someone here who's made it
look at the scars on my skin
and know that they run
all the way through

but i'm still here
and so are you

GASOLINE

dad,

before i found my voice
i would wait by the door
late, chilly
until you got home
you'd smell of
gasoline
thick coveralls
rough against my skin
i didn't care
that you were silent
that you were too tired
to ask me how my day was
i didn't care
because i wanted to be
just like you

you are wise, dad
you have a wisdom about you
and even though
you don't say much
i have always trusted your word
as true
but the truth is

some of the most painful scars i bear
are from words you threw
like a discarded cigarette
still lit
lighting fire to
the traces of gasoline
left on my skin

you never said much
but when you did
i believed it like the gospel
i believed that someone who was sparse
with their words
would only take the pains to speak
if it was the absolute truth

you don't say much
but once you told me
that i couldn't possibly annoy you
because you weren't listening to me anyway

from that moment on
i believed that my voice could be
loud and grating
incessant and energetic
the only sound in the small space of the car—

but still, no one would hear me.

i'm not listening to you anyway
a throwaway comment
not meant to injure
harmless, now that i'm older
harmless as a discarded cigarette
still lit
carelessly thrown onto
the gasoline traces
that i collected like
ariel's cove of treasures
in the most vulnerable
hollows of my heart

i didn't know then
the strength of my own voice
so i fell silent

listen to me now
i love you
i'm grateful
because, in the grand scheme of things
i am still here
i have every material blessing
i have a house a car a dog and
enough food for two of me
i am blessed that
you stayed
i am blessed that

you never used stick or stone
to hurt me

only words

in the grand scheme of things
your words weren't supposed to hurt
and maybe that's my fault
for believing you
for trading in my voice
so i could be
just like you
i don't blame you anymore
i forgive you
i have reclaimed my voice
and i thank you
because if it weren't for you
i never would have found
the strength of my voice
through writing

i don't say much
but when i do
i try to find ways
to make my words soothe
the gasoline burns of others
with scars just like mine

i hope you can hear me now

CLOTH MOTHER

it is said
when children are young
they can learn any language
as long as they hear
enough syllables
to make up all the words

it is also said
that love
has many languages
    words of affirmation
    gifts
    acts of service
    quality time
    physical touch
i think there are more
    food
    discipline
    hard work
    boundaries
    honesty
    probably more
but those ones take longer
to learn

it is said
that if a baby monkey
grows up in a cage
with a *wire* mother
    who supplies them with food
and a *cloth* mother
    who provides them with comfort
if given a choice, the baby monkey will run to
the cloth mother
every time

if another baby monkey
grows up in another cage
with a wire mother
    who provides plenty of food for sustenance
but with no cloth mother at all
    no one to run to when they are scared
    no one to cling to when the lightning strikes
        that baby monkey
            grows up
                      anxious
     distant
          fearful
                     unable
                            to
cope.

it is said

    that love

        has many languages

and young children

    will only learn

        whatever syllables

are said out loud

FILL IN THE

i choose my words
carefully

sometimes
there are gaps
               in my
                       speech
periods of pause
during which i am selecting
      the exact words
      the proper tone
to convey my meaning

i know it's tempting
but don't interrupt

because words have power
and i want you to experience
the force of mine

it's difficult to express myself
when it comes to you
it's near impossible
to find the words
to appropriately describe
the chaos of emotions whirring inside

it's a challenge i have decided is worth
spending the rest of my life
attempting to conquer

but sometimes

words fail

and all there is, is _____

just know that i tried

sometimes, i will use other words
to express what i'm feeling
how are you
can i help
i hope you are doing okay
sometimes, you may have to
accept silence
as the only sound you will get from these lips
sometimes, you will have to
fill in the _____
because i will have trouble
filling it in myself

i'm working on it
i'm trying to be
                      forthcoming

so here it is, in its simplest form:

i love you
          i do

and i wanted you to know
you don't have to imagine
you won't have to doubt
for just this once, you don't have to

fill in the _____

please know
i don't say those words lightly
i am overflowing with it
i hope you will understand
when i am
          quiet
when words
          fail
this is what i want to say:

i love you
          i really really do

it comes with no expectation
you don't have to reciprocate
i just needed you to know

christina lee

in case no one has ever said
those words to you before

here it is again:

(wait for the pause

because i want you to experience
the force of my words)

i love you.
                i love you.
                              i love you.

please, fill in the _____

QUIVER

there is a wound
deep inside your heart
for years
you've covered it with
cotton bandages
layer upon layer
without daring to see
the damage underneath
but

can't you smell that horrible rot?

i know it hurts
it has
for years
you say it doesn't
but every time someone tries
to get close
you flinch away
because even the gentlest touch
can cause pain for days

it's time to cut away
the dead tissue

can't you tell it's festering?

there is a poisonous injury
deep in your core
something horrible
is lodged in the softness there
nothing blooms
in the shadow of that
broken arrow
sticking out like
an invisible splinter
it's unbearable
but it's got to come out
the same way it went in

pull hard
be gentle
deep breath
and when you exhale
the worst will be over

there is healing
on the horizon
the worst is over
but that doesn't mean
this part isn't going to be painful
healing is slow
and sometimes you must
reset the bone
that has fused incorrectly

this might hurt worse
than the original injury
deep breath
exhale

crack open that
positive spirit
you'll see the rays of dawn
breaking through
the bottom of the bottle

there is a thick pulse
deep inside your heart
breathing, living
you are alive
you are alive
you are alive
blood is a comforting warmth
red with oxygen, with sunlight
it means
you are alive
you have all you need
so deep breath
exhale

we are still here

WAR

put down your swords
the war is over
your enemies are
imaginary friends
you should have shed
long ago

pull off the blindfold
the night is peaceful
the clouds have all disappeared
and all that is left is
a gentle breeze, warm
and a beautiful crescent moon

lay down your walls
there's nothing left to defend
you're strong enough
to let people in
real strength is trusting someone
to let them close enough
to kill you

take a deep breath
no one can hurt you now
because you've learned that hurt
is just a sign of growth

pulling
stretching
moulding
no pain will hurt enough
to kill you

so put down the blades
pull off your armor
lay down your defenses
and be brave
be weak
be open
to the possibility of pain
for the guarantee
of happiness

BEANSPROUT

yes, i've grown
taller, sure
wider, of course
yes, you could say
i've grown
but maybe
i'm a beansprout
pale and flimsy
without leaves
growing endlessly
in the dark

i know this is not
where i'm meant to be
but part of me feels
too old, too stuck
to re-learn and learn from
my mistakes
i'm too comfortable
to grow through the pains
all over again
yes, i've grown
complacent at the top
and cutting me back down to size
is a twenty-seven-foot drop

but as my dad would say
pruning only helps a plant grow

you can't be strong
unless you're pushing back
against something that is trying
to crush you

there comes a point
where you can't point the blame
at anyone but yourself

i'm a coward
i'm well aware
can't blame this on
a missing heart
i'm untested
too scared to seek out
something that might
crush my fragile spine
just a sad little beansprout
hiding in the dark
because my skin, it's pale
and at first touch
the sun is going to burn

but

i'm sick of living in the dark
i'm sick of pretending like
i've grown
when all i've done is
stretch myself thin

i see you, sun

here are my yellow hands
turn them into green leaves
or thin bristles
or maidenhair fans

here is my fragile spine
break it and rebuild it
until it is hardened wood
reveal to me what kind of tree i am

here, i'm just a beansprout
shine on me, sun
and show me how much it hurts
to grow in the light

# VOLUME II:

METAMORPHOSIS

TREAD SOFTLY

in mount pleasant cemetery
there is a plaque that reads
"tread softly,
a dream lies
sleeping here"

which, at first
sounds nice
a sleeping dream

but
slumbering, a dream
is cotton-candy clouds
a lullaby that can only be uttered
in the dark safety of sheets

but what happens
when sleeping dreams wake?
let's see
tread softly
and see if you can coax
that sleeping dream out into the sun
sing gently
tread softly
and see what comes sauntering out
from under the brush

it's coming out of hibernation
feed it gradually
keep your hands around it
until it is strong enough
to withstand the next gust of wind
then give it room to grow
some space to burn
let it hunt for survival
in the dark recesses where you are
too afraid to go

tread softly
and let your sleeping dream
wake slowly
let it see the sunrise
let it open its wings
and fly off into
the sunset
and then
once it has run its course
once it has blazed a path
across your heart and
lit up all those dusty corners
only then will it
tread softly
back to its resting place
a dream asleep
sleeping softly

YOU'RE A WIZARD, HARRY

i believe in magic
in moments touched
by the visit of something
wondrous
tangible electricity
electrical energy
whizzing through the air
did you feel that?
that jolt in your chest
there it was
proof it was here
the impossible made a dent
in the beat of your life force

that is magic

if magic is defined
as anything that can't be explained
by science
admit it
you want to believe it, too
that there are some things
we will never explain
with a clever theory
some significant numbers
and a tight conclusion

some things are magical
because they cannot be caught
by the nets
of our limiting thinking

that is magic

your perception is
your reality
just because it's all in your head
doesn't mean it's not real
if perception is
your reality
why wouldn't you choose
to believe in magic?

THE SKY

a box has
four corners
four straight walls
meant to keep things out

a box
keeps you contained
easily stacked on top of one another
neatly stored
set aside
forgotten treasures lost inside

sometimes they have windows
crack it open once in while
so you can feel the wind on your skin

i don't understand religions where
they worship god from inside a box
god lives in the sky
no barriers from
the sea, wind and rain

boxes don't exist in nature
they were created by man
to keep other men from
breaking free

break free
and see what lays beyond
the brick and mortar
take a fucking breath
because your lungs
have been breathing in
stale air for years

imagine yourself
a bird
the sky has
no corners
no walls to contain
whatever whim
whatever current
whatever flap of your wings
you choose

four corners is
four too many

you deserve the sky

CANNABIS

it is bad, i know
but i like how it makes me
sit straighter in my spine
like my sleepy old skeleton
has finally clicked into
the right connection
it's like the smoke
opened a blocked portal
to the rest of my body
i was stuck inside my head
but just *inhale, exhale*
and now i have limbs
a body that *moves*
and *breathes*
and *aches*
i like feeling every
crick in my joints
clack into place
wrist
elbow
shoulder
unclench that jaw
ahh, right there
don't you dare
move a muscle

it is bad
i know
but i like how i can feel
the curious tingle of blood tickling
my neglected neurons
random rollercoasters of
imagination
screaming new life
into old thoughts
purged like
broken piñatas
scattering past pains and hurts
like crisp leaves
crunched. on. concrete.
the secret of my thought patterns
was lost to me
until the smoke
burnt up
all the ways in which
i was holding myself back

it is bad
i know
but i like that it calms me down
remember—
all those sleepless nights
when i'd wear down the springs in my mattress
with my thoughts, bouncing

around the room
remember those endless spirals
paralyzed in a wormhole
of my own making—
yeah, i don't remember
it makes me forget
and i like that i don't remember
that there was anything
to be worried about
before the smoke

it is bad, i know
but i like how it sets my soul
ablaze
too electric
for this stretchy skin
itching
begging
please
for sweet sweet release
for once i want to please
my body instead of
my brain
i am hot helium
and this human habit
is a balloon stretched taut—
the hindenburg
set to burst

it is bad
(i know)

but it helped bring back
my voice
i can't help but sing
to every song that rings
through my body
oh, birds flying high
you know how i feel
Nina Simone zings
straight through my soul
it's a new dawn
it's a new day
it's a new life for me
and i'm feeling—
my heart erupts from
my scorched throat
oh, that sweet acrid smoke
makes me sing much too loud
to be courteous to the neighbours

oh lord
it is bad

…or is it?
can it be bad
if for the first time

in a long time
i remember
what it feels like to be
...happy?

huh
so that is the difference
between living
and surviving

this is bad
i know
the freed thoughts
inside my brain
the delicious pleasure
inside my skin
the rampant racing of
my once stagnant heart
it's too much

but it makes me feel
Divine, capital D
Holy
Goddess

can you believe
i've lived centuries
within months

yes, i've grown
(but i'm a beansprout in the Dark)

it is bad, trust me
I KNOW
i'm dependent
on this newfound confidence
to be myself

i'm scared to lose me
to that shy self-conscious girl
i was before
i'm in need of some
rest and relaxation
from my own
arresting thoughts
arresting my development
into the woman
i am now

it is bad, i know
but i'm afraid
to let it go

it is bad
very bad
but maybe

it is good...
it is good enough...
it is just for now
    not forever
    just until
i can muster enough
courage and
self-love
to be myself
while sober[*]

---

[*] *at the time of publication, the author has been over a year sober, and damn proud of herself*

GALAXY, PART I

i imagine
a soul is like
a galaxy
billions of stars mixed together
to create a sum
that is greater
than its parts

sometimes it feels like
part of my soul broke free
whirring through the universe
untethered
leaving a broken jagged edge
        a black vacuum
                where stars used to shine
     at the border of my consciousness
imagine the glory
the awe-inspiring alignment
of a soul fragment returning
            fusing
        merging once again

light, where there was once only
        jagged black vacuum

GALAXY, PART II

imagine
if two souls combined
to become indistinguishable
two galaxies
so compatible that they merge
without destroying the other
two souls
that combine so completely
they are now made
of the same stuff
a new entity made from
infinite stars
that revolve around each other
in new and unpredictable
trajectories

their sum
        greater than
                their parts

the merging of two galaxies
should happen slowly
a brush of two stars
      at the jagged broken edges
a gradual ombre of overlap
a blurring of boundaries

until a threshold
                —invisible, intangible—
is reached
a slow process with a quick conclusion
until we no longer know
which star came from where

how marvelous
how terrifying it would be
to lose oneself
in someone else's stars

MAYBE A FOREST IS A BETTER METAPHOR

did you know
there are more trees on planet earth
than stars in the milky way?

unbelievable
but it's true

unexpected
but i like it

A FANTASY

we're standing on the balcony
your shoulder touching mine
our legs line up
    like bowling pins
    that will never be knocked down
you don't have to ask
what i'm thinking
you wrap your arm around me
and both of us
exhale
the space between us
we are a perfect fit

all is still

the skies turn pink with pleasure
because we have finally found
the person with whom
to watch the sun set
to greet the moon rise
as the stars scatter above us

how marvelous
how terrifying it would be
to lose myself
in all your stars

BREADCRUMBS

i hate to sound needy
but i need to know
how are you?
how do you feel?
about me?
i'm oversensitive
i make big fragrant loafs
out of the breadcrumbs
you've left me
i pick them up off the ground
and inflate them with my imaginations
until they are grandiose and porous in my stomach
fooling myself into thinking
they are enough to feed me

i hate to sound demanding
but i demand better than this
i'm a desert flower
i've learned to grow bristles
to protect me from the drought
but i demand
just enough water
to survive these mental sand storms

i hate these hopeless images
that keep imagining themselves

across shuttered eyelids
pictures of you and i
that don't exist
pink-tinged snippets
of how our lives could be
i'm caught
in a daydream snare
nostalgic for
an impossible future

i hate how little of you
my heart needed
to completely latch onto
barely a few seconds of my day
and already it feels like
no one else could compare
to nothing but
fucking breadcrumbs
a full course meal
stands on the other side
of deflated promises
but i am too frail
        too weak
to drag myself past you

i hate this hunger
in my core
this is not healthy behavior

my hand, trembling
scrawls love poems
you'll never read
    i'll never send
and i, a brainless bird,
will keep pecking at the pavement
damaging my skull
for just another taste of
fucking breadcrumbs

i hate that you have somebody else
today, green is my favorite color
because when i put it on
it brings out the red in my skin tone
burning hot
at the thought
of you in the arms
of someone who is not me

i hate that i've wasted
all these blank pages
filled them with words you'll never read
                    i'll never send
these blank pages
must forever bear the brunt
of my darkest desires
   my unforgiving addiction
this sad sad part of my heart

that begs me to just be satisfied
with nothing but
breadcrumbs

(i hate this insatiable ghost
the one that grew up believing
that these stale breadcrumbs
are all that i deserve)

i hate this empty space beside me
a white silhouette drawn on pavement
one that is shaped just like you
how much longer until i realize
that breadcrumbs will never be enough
to make a person whole?

but the thing i hate most of all
is that i've left a trail of breadcrumbs
just enough for you
to find your way here

tell me one thing
did you mean for me to follow
those breadcrumbs you left behind or
are you just a messy eater?

IS THIS POEM ABOUT DRUGS OR HIM

i'm giving you up
probably
i mean,

i'm going to try
to give you up
because i've wasted
too many sighs
over you
enough breath
to last me years

probably

it's a hyperbole
i've been dancing
on this hyperbolic arch
that puts you at the peak
and i'm getting
motion-sick

so i'm going
(to try)
to give you up

sigh.
this is harder than i thought
and i haven't even started yet
thoughts of you
are exiting my system
and i already want
to inhale you
all over again
i need

to give you up

it is bad
for my blackened lungs
breathing in
toxic fumes
so i'm coughing you
out of my throat
i'm choking on you

i am giving you up

sigh.
probably.

IMPRISONED

when we embrace
our hearts realize
they are trapped
inside a prison

separated by
red walls
white bars
a cage where
the only source
of communication
is the soft
knock-knock
ba-dum ba-dum
the life force
keeping our hearts in tune

when we embrace
our hearts ask
through their flesh prisons
are you there?
it's been days
since we last spoke

DARK CHOCOLATE

all sighs are dark chocolate
        bittersweet

VOLCANO

you don't even know
what love is

quell those juvenile fantasies
    those childish beliefs
that love, when it comes,
will feel like what you read in a book
those are fiction
flattened play things
add one more dimension
and see how messy
complicated
love gets

if you're being honest
you don't really want love
you're far too comfortable
being on your own
nobody to lean on
no one to get too close, to see
    the pores on your face
    the valleys of your skin
    the fault lines running deep through

your heart
is a volcano, dormant

crusted over with
black rock
leftover from an eruption long ago
when was the last time
that lava ran hot?
red and angry?
that's not
what it's supposed to feel like, you say
or is it?

how would you even know?

purge yourself
of those ridiculous fantasies
where the prince comes riding in
and kills the dragon keeping your heart locked
inside a volcano
because the truth is
that dragon is you
you are the one breathing fire
at anyone who tries to get
too close
then you lash out, angry
because no one is brave enough
to slay you

pull yourself together

those stories have rotted your teeth
you're malnourished
from eating spun sugar all day
i'm not telling you not to dream
but make sure you can tell the difference between
being awake and
being comatose
you don't even know the difference, do you?

it might be nice for a while
living in this utopian world
but eventually
the darkness is going to seep up
from underneath those
flattened shallow landscapes
get a grip
get your hands dirty
trees can only grow
if their roots go deep enough
pull on that loose thread
the stitches are ready to come out
the tissue is still raw, yes
but it'll never heal
unless it bleeds a little

you don't even know
what it's like
to let someone fill their hands

with all your dirt
to let them leave fingerprints
  all over those walls you've kept clean
  those barriers you've built
  to barricade yourself from other people's shit

but how will you ever know
what love is
from inside a sterile prison?

it's going to hurt
i'm warning you now
but you already know about pain
and you're still here
move on
move along
there is nothing left here
for you to see

it is time
for you to relinquish your hold
on being safe inside
this haunted diorama you built
to keep people out
tame your own damn dragon
and ride it away from this volcano
that's kept you trapped for so long

it is time
to write your own stories
make them messy
complicated
live with dirt on your hands
and watch as the roots take hold
you never know
turn that inhospitable black rock
into verdant green

you don't even know
what love is

SNAKE

the old skins
are peeling off me
in flakes
i am changed, see?
but when i'm with you
i feel like i must put on
the old dead skin of my youth
i've outgrown
this masquerade where we pretend to be
the hurt children of the past
i am different, see?
i don't want to be stuck
in this ouroboros
of misery, anymore

don't put me back in the box
from which i just broke free
can't you see the struggle it was
to break out of that
wretched skin?
let me transform
i want to be born anew

forget what you thought
you knew about me

give me room to rediscover
how to move around
in this new suit
it won't be pretty

but no one said you had to watch

CANYON

i'm sorry i've put
                                                  this distance
between us
but the ground upon which we stand
has grown apart
a canyon, yawning wide
we have built a bridge
made of memories
but we can only cross
when nostalgia comes knocking

we can't live on a bridge forever

i'm sorry this hurts so much
maybe it would be less painful
if i had stayed
but the stagnation was a chisel
chipping away
at my marble heart
into something
permanently damaged

i'm sorry i can't explain
what i'm feeling
i'm sorry that the only words
i know how to say

are the ones i tell these pages

i can't shout across a canyon
but maybe one day
my voice will be loud enough
for you to hear the words
i'm screaming across
                      this gaping void:

                                      i'm sorry
                                      i love you
                                    i thank you

                              but i am happier here
                                  on the other side
                                    of this canyon.

DEAR ME, PART I

dear christina
dearly beloved me
i'm going to lay it out clearly for you
because clearly
this will only reach you
if it's written out clearly for you

there only exists
one of you
that's the truth

but there also exists
a photocopy of you
inside the brains of everyone you know

you, but faded
you, but grainy black-and-white
you, but flawed in some way
    due to a malfunction
    in *their* viewfinder

there exists
a version of you
in the minds of everyone around

and you have no control over
how other people take
a flawed picture of your soul

so you shouldn't waste your time
trying to color correct
for someone else's
blurry viewfinder

DEAR ME, PART II

you're not a chameleon
forever shifting
to satisfy everyone else's
favorite colors

worn-denim blues
rusted orange
linen beige
morning yellow
chloroplast green
that's you

who cares
if they don't match?

CARBON

my favorite thing in the world
is watching my dog eat
i understand now
why my grandmother was
always shoveling food onto our plates

we named him Carbon
one of the most important elements
for organic life
there's a whole field of science
dedicated to
the chemistry of carbon
how it bonds
how it breaks
how it forms the structures necessary
for living

Carbon loves apples
and carrots
and even the hard white parts
of romaine lettuce
what a weird dog
one of those rare vegans
he quivers with excitement
every time we say the word
a-p-p-l-e

that we had to start spelling it out
in normal conversation
so not to trigger him
Pavlov would have been proud

i could go on about all the things
that make me love Carbon
but i won't, just to spare you
i know it's weird
to write a love poem about a dog
but Carbon
took that inorganic matter
lifeless inside my chest
and transformed it into
a living, breathing organ

once i was watching him eat
and i started to cry
because i imagined a time when
i wouldn't get to watch him eat anymore
when his joints will hurt too much
to jump up and greet me at the door
when he won't want to
play with any of his toys

i understand now
why i was so afraid of love before

it's scary
to love so much
that you cry while watching a dog eat
what the fuck?
what the fuck kind of sickness is this?
in life there is always balance
which means
it's going to hurt just as bad
as the good feels
once it's gone
but
i wouldn't be here, now
if it weren't for my sweet baby boy
my heart would still be
crusted over
a dormant volcano
inorganic matter

but now, my heart
it bleeds
and cries
and aches
and breaks—
and laughs
and wants
and shares
and *loves*

it's scary to be alive
but Carbon showed me how
he's one of the most important elements
of life
and i don't care
if you think it's weird
that i wrote a poem for my dog
because i could write
a whole field of science
on why
on how much
on all the different ways that
i love my dog

he is my heart
and i'm not afraid of love
anymore

MYSELF

all these poems are
for me

for the girl who was afraid
to be herself
god, i love her
she made it through
second by second
minute by minute
day by day
and every single time
she felt like giving in
she stood firm
she grew stronger
and look how much her leaves
have grown in

all these poems are
for the woman who is becoming
she is nowhere near perfect
but what tree ever is
turns out she's an evergreen
dress her up in lights
and she'll bring joy even on
the coldest nights

all these poems are
for the legend she will become
she'll be a garden
a place of peace and love and beauty
and she's never going to stop growing
until her roots burst right through the concrete
until a canopy of leaves hangs above you
giving shade to rest your head

all these poems are
for myself
and through writing them
i fell in love
with me

GREENSPACE

i wrote these poems
in the greenspaces
around Toronto
i walked for hours
with my notebook and pen
in the heat of the summer
amongst the trees and their shade

it was the best summer of my life
because i finally confronted
the pain that lived in my heart
for so long
i realized that i felt so alone
because i refused to let anyone see
how much i had
fallen apart on the inside

those greenspaces
saved my life
when i was lost
and hurt
and confused
and alone
they reminded me that
there is always a tree to lean on
a patch of lush grass to sit upon

and flowers to show you that
life is beautiful
it really is
even when it isn't

i am free now
because of those
greenspaces

harbourfront
spadina museum
wychwood artscape
a balcony on bloor street
riverdale park
trinity bellwoods
budapest park
grange park
canoe landing
nathan phillips
armstrong redwoods national park (california)
toronto music garden
philosopher's walk
queen's park

and even when it snows
in the streets of Toronto
i will cherish
those warm summer days

sitting by the lake
and feeling the peace
      and the knowing that:
i am not alone
i am not imprisoned
i am loved
and i deserve the sky

TRANSFORMATION

hello, little one
we have come to the end
of another cycle
it is time now
to pull yourself out of the darkness
no longer a frail little beansprout
but a redwood
pointing up towards the sun

now comes the growing part

we are at
another end
i am king arthur
queen of hearts
removing rusted swords
from frostbitten stone
my heart is
black and blue
tinged with greens
brushed with yellows

bruised
but healing

some days i think
god, when will this war be over
i thought i dealt with this already
but the truth is
grievous injuries are
always on the horizon
because pain is not a thing
to be avoided

happiness is the light
to pain's darkness
one can't exist
without the other

when once i would have focused
only on the pain
now i choose to see the other side

happiness is
letting someone see
the wound inside of you
and trusting that they won't do
more damage
to the bruises
someone else left behind

happiness is
watching a dog eat apples

standing amongst ancient trees
growing your own greenhouse
to keep those greenspaces with you

happiness is not being afraid
to share your voice
to sing so loudly
that other people are annoyed
but you do it anyway
it is, finally, for once
being stronger than
the voices in your head
telling you
you're not good enough
listen to me
you are good enough
you are more than enough
you matter
remember

happiness is
being so in love with yourself
that no one else matters

happiness is
knowing you're loved
by you.

ACKNOWLEDGEMENTS

thank you for reading this collection
i am grateful to you for making it this far

thank you to:
my sisters, Abigail and Rebecca
i wouldn't be who i am without you
my parents, for listening
my grandparents, for being the foundation
Gomo, for being an artist and creator
Carbon, my sweetest baby boy

Yi-Yi, i trust your judgment on all things:
good, bad, bad-in-a-good-way, and truly bad
Monica, for showing me the brain
and for always willing to explore it with me
Andrea, my sister from another mister
i can't wait to drink with you in Australia
Ori, my oldest and truest friend
i look forward to us as old ladies
Rob, you showed me it is safe to be myself
and i will always love you for that (and more)

to Rozlyn Dubz
for creating the best cover
to Harry Potter
for proving that magic is possible
to BTS
for telling me to love myself until i finally listened
to all the artists
for creating beautiful things

thank you.

About the Author

Christina Lee is a poet and writer living in the Toronto area. She has been blessed with many opportunities, such as graduate school, living in Milan as an *au pair*, teaching high school math and science, and many other exciting ventures. She has always been interested in psychology, art, literature, self-exploration, and how all those things come together. This is her first published poetry collection.

Book Cover Credits

Rozlyn Dubz
@rozlyndubztattoos
www.rozlyndubz.com